MW01051872

Modern Rhymes About Ancient Times

ANCIENT ROME

Written by Susan Altman and Susan Lechner

Illustrated by Sue Hughes

Children's Press®
A Division of Scholastic Inc.
New York • Toronto • London • Auckland • Sydney
Mexico City • New Delhi • Hong Kong
Danbury, Connecticut

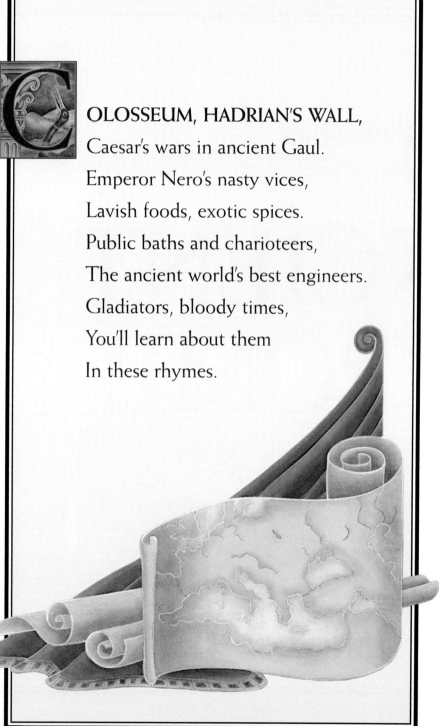

COLOSSEUM, HADRIAN'S WALL,

Caesar's wars in ancient Gaul.

Emperor Nero's nasty vices,

Lavish foods, exotic spices.

Public baths and charioteers,

The ancient world's best engineers.

Gladiators, bloody times,

You'll learn about them

In these rhymes.

With much love to James and Jessica—my own choice for empire builders.—S. R. A.

To Jack and Sam—we who are about to be published salute you—with much love. And a special, loving salute to Maude Maser Lechner—the most wonderful granddaughter in ancient or modern times.—S. L.

Reading Consultant: Nanci Vargus, Ed.D., Decatur Township Schools, Indianapolis, Indiana

Book production by Editorial Directions, Inc.

Book design by Marie O'Neill

Library of Congress Cataloging-in-Publication Data
Altman, Susan.
  Ancient Rome / written by Susan Altman and Susan Lechner ; illustrated by Sue Hughes.
    p. cm. — (Modern rhymes about ancient times)
    ISBN 0-516-21148-X (lib. bdg.) 0-516-27374-4 (pbk.)
    1. Rome—Juvenile poetry. 2. History, Ancient—Juvenile poetry. 3. Children's poetry, American. [1. Rome—Civilization—Poetry. 2. American poetry.]
I. Lechner, Susan. II. Hughes, Sue, ill. III. Series.
    PS3551.L7943 A85 2001
    811'.54—dc21   2001028232

TABLE OF CONTENTS

THE SEVEN HILLS OF ROME

Rome was built on seven hills.
Each hill had a name.
See if you can learn them—
Pretend that it's a game.

The Viminal (*VIM-in-ill*)
The Aventine (*AV-in-tine*)
The Quirinal (*KWIR-in-ill*)
The Esquiline (*ES-kwe-line*)

To these please add the
Palatine (*PAL-uh-tine*)
The Caelian (*SEE-lee-in*)
The Capitoline. (*CAP-it-oh-line*)

Rome was built on seven hills
And there begins the story
Of the famous Roman Empire
And its eternal glory.

While the city of Rome was built on just seven hills, the Roman Empire eventually extended to much of Europe, the Middle East, and North Africa.

REMUS AND ROMULUS

Remus and Romulus
Where have you been?
"Out in the forest,
A wolf took us in."

"She fed us and nursed us,
Just like her own,
Then gave us to shepherds
Until we were grown."

Remus and Romulus
What will you be?
"The founders of Rome
Seven five three B.C."

Remus is pronounced REE-mus. *Romulus* is pronounced ROM-u-lus.

THE ROMAN ARMY

The Roman army legions conquered all those in their path.

And every country feared to be the target of their wrath.

Courageous, strong and disciplined, trained to march and fight.

They terrified their enemies with overwhelming might.

They brought back wagons full of slaves and treasures from each war.

Because of them the Romans ruled from shore to distant shore.

ROMAN ROADS

The ancients used to say
That "all roads lead to Rome."
The Romans needed many roads
To bring their soldiers home.

They marched away to conquer,
They dealt in foreign trade,
They traveled on vacation,
They strutted on parade.

To all their distant provinces,
Those roads ran long and straight.
They made the Roman Empire
Glorious and great.

8

THE FORUM

In the Forum they would talk, converse, discuss.

In the Forum they would argue, even cuss.

In the Forum they'd debate,

Scheme, make plans, pontificate,

And analyze at length affairs of state.

In the Forum you could hear a lively speech.

All the senators were right within your reach.

You could hear the latest news,

Pay attention, or just snooze,

Or stand up and give the leaders your own views.

The Forum was the public square of ancient Rome.

UBLIC BATHS

It's hard to be clean
With no plumbing at home,
But that was no problem
For people in Rome.

They built public baths
That were lavishly planned,
Models of luxury,
Splendid and grand.

There were hot rooms
And steam rooms
And pools that were cold,
Tubs made of marble
With faucets of gold.

There were gardens and terraces,
Rooms of all sorts,
Libraries,
Reading rooms,
Spaces for sports.

Friends met with friends.
It was quite a routine.
They had a great time,
And they also got clean.

TOGA

The Roman man
Was simply dressed.
No suit, no tie,
No pants, no vest.

The toga was made of
A white woolen sheet.
It fell in folds
From neck to feet.

A sign of the Empire,
Known worldwide,
The Roman toga—
Worn with pride!

Toga is pronounced TOE-guh.

A ROMAN DINNER PARTY

Lie down when you eat?
That really sounds neat.
That's just how the Romans ate dinner.
You'd lie on your side
On a couch low and wide.
(Not easy if you're a beginner.)

You'd reach with your hand
For the food on a stand.
No need for a fork, spoon, or knife.
Dish followed dish,
Have a fig! Have a fish!
It was really a rather nice life.

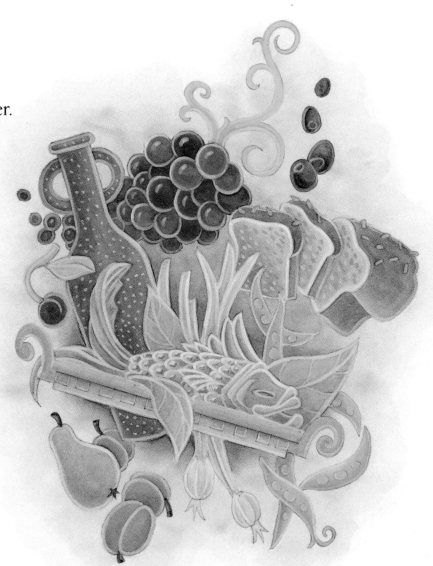

OMAN NUMERALS

Some letters led a double life.
They served as numbers, too.
They used a simple system—
The numerals were few.

For one you used the letter "I."
For five the letter "V."
"L" was fifty; "X" was ten.
One hundred was a "C."

The system had its problems though,
When numbers got too high.
And Romans weren't able
To divide or multiply.

Their numerals were useful
But it's very clear to me,
That we are served much better
By our numbers 1, 2, 3, . . .

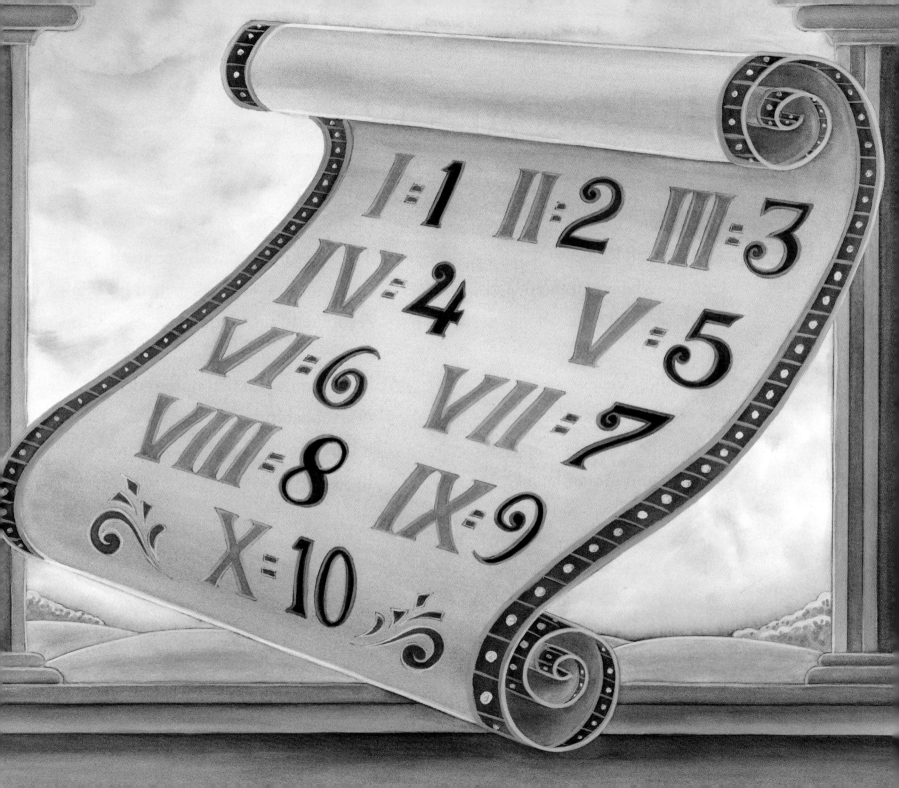

JULIUS CAESAR (100–44 B.C.)

Caesar, mighty Caesar,
A hero to all Rome,
Conquered many foreign lands,
Impressing folks back home.

"Veni, Vidi, Vici,"
He said with great elation.
Or "I came, I saw, I conquered."
(That's Latin in translation.)

He fixed the Roman calendar,
The dates marked with precision.
One month—July—is named for him—
A tribute to his vision.

His enemies stabbed him to death,
A great catastrophe.
It happened on the Ides of March,
In 44 B.C.

The Ides of March fell on the fifteenth day of the month in the Roman calendar.

CROSSING THE RUBICON RIVER  (49 B.C.)

Caesar had great power,

But still he wanted more.

And if he crossed the Rubicon

He knew there would be war.

"Stay in Gaul," the Senate said.

"Do not come back to Rome.

Keep your army up in Gaul.

Don't think of coming home."

Caesar thought for several days,

Then made his move at last.

He marched his army right across

And said, "The die is cast."

Rubicon is pronounced ROO-buh-con. Gaul was the Roman name for what is now France and part of Germany. A die is one of a pair of dice. In many games, once you throw the dice, you have taken your turn and cannot undo it. When Julius Caesar said, "The die is cast," he meant that by crossing the Rubicon River he had disobeyed the Roman Senate and that it was too late to turn back.

POMPEY (106–48 B.C.)

Pompey was a general.
Pompey had great power.
But when he clashed with Caesar,
His life turned very sour.

When they fought a Civil War,
Pompey's hopes were stilled.
Pompey fled to Egypt,
Where Caesar had him killed.

Pompey is pronounced POM-pee.

# NERO (A.D. 37–68)

Emperor Nero
Was no hero.
An evil man was he.

With Rome on fire,
He played his lyre,
And laughed with fiendish glee.

He killed his mother,
And his brother.
He also killed his wife.

Nero's rule
Was hard and cruel.
He led an evil life.

Nero is pronounced NEAR-oh.
A lyre is a musical instrument.

THE PRAETORIAN GUARDS

The Praetorian guards were lean and mean,
The emperor's personal army.
The Roman emperor bragged to his friends,
"They'll never let anyone harm me."

The Praetorian guards kept gaining more power.
Their influence grew ever stronger.
One day the guards, quite scornfully said,
"We're protecting the emperor no longer."

The Praetorian guards, once loyal and true,
Turned traitor—a real about-face.
They killed any emperor they didn't like,
And chose who would rule in his place.

Praetorian is pronounced pre-TORE-ee-un.

24

LADIATORS

They fought with sword
And spear and net.
The watching crowd
Would cheer and bet.

They fought with skill
Till their last breath,
Because they fought
Until the death.

They fought wild beasts;
They fought each other;
They'd fight a friend;
They'd fight a brother.

Their lives were hard,
And often short.
They spilled their blood,
And called it sport.

HE CIRCUS MAXIMUS

In chariot races perilous
The fearless drivers glorious
Strive to be victorious
As at the Circus Maximus
Around and round they go.

The cheering crowds roar thunderous
Applause for athletes valorous
A spectacle quite fabulous
When at the Circus Maximus
Around and round they go.

Around and round they go.
Around and round they go.
Around . . . and round . . . and round . . . they go.

Maximus is pronounced MAX-ih-muss.

PARTACUS (Died 71 B.C.)

There once was a man named Spartacus
Who stirred up an enormous fuss.
Oh yes! Oh yes, he did!

A gladiator, brave and bold,
He wouldn't do as he was told.
Oh no! Oh no, he wouldn't!

He led the slaves in a revolt.
It gave the Romans quite a jolt.
Oh yes! Oh yes, it did!

And though he died so long ago,
His story lives for those who know
That freedom is a wondrous thing,
A magic bird as it takes wing,
Hard to catch and hard to hold,
To be valued more than gold,
Guaranteed to all of us
By those who dare,
Like Spartacus.

Oh yes!

Spartacus is pronounced SPAR-tuh-cuss.

28

HANNIBAL (247–183 B.C.)

Hannibal and his elephants
Came marching, marching, marching.
Hannibal and his elephants
Came marching over the Alps.

They marched to fight the Romans
In the streets and in the fields,
With spears and clubs and javelins,
With arrows, swords, and shields.

Hannibal and his elephants
Came marching, marching, marching.
Hannibal and his elephants
Came marching over the Alps.

This general from Carthage
Fighting far from home,
Won battle after battle,
But he couldn't conquer Rome.

Hannibal and his elephants
Came marching, marching, marching.
Hannibal and his elephants
Came marching over the Alps.

The best thing 'bout traveling with elephants
As opposed to a donkey or skunk—
You don't have to buy extra luggage
Since elephants come with a trunk.

THE PLANETS

There's Jupiter, Mercury,
Pluto and Mars,
Venus and Neptune,
Surrounded by stars.

Saturn, Uranus,
They all have their place,
Orbiting endlessly
Way out in space.

As they're in the heavens,
It doesn't seem odd,
That each of these planets
Was named for a god.

The Romans had many gods and goddesses. The planets are named after the more important ones.

THE VESTALS

The fire,
Sacred fire,
Must be guarded
Day and night.
The Vestals
Had that duty
And they had
To do it right.

The Vestals—
Pure young women—
Followed
Every rule.
Models
Of behavior,
They could never
Lose their cool.

The Vestals—
There were six of them—
Performed their work
With pride.
Their main regret was
None of them
Could ever
Be a bride.

# AQUEDUCTS

There was water in the hillsides,
But not enough in town,
The Romans found a clever way
To bring that water down.

"Aqueducts" they called them.
The concept was quite new—
Arches topped with channels,
To run the water through.

The water came from streams and lakes,
From places far away.
Engineering marvels!
Some still exist today.

Aqueduct is pronounced AH-kwuh-dukt.

OMPEII

The sun was warm that summer day
Life was good in old Pompeii.

Children played beneath a fountain
No one thought about the mountain.

Then BOOM!
DOOM!

Mount Vesuvius blew its top!
The dreadful noise just wouldn't stop.

Flames shot up two hundred feet.
People panicked in the street!

Smoke and ash blacked out the sun
And everyone began to run.

Poison gas poured down the hill.
People choked and then lay still.

Burning ashes filled the sky,
And formed a blanket twelve feet high.

Pompeii was gone. No trace remained.
Vesuvius
Had been unchained.

Pompeii is pronounced pom-PAY. *Vesuvius* is pronounced vuh-SOO-vee-us.

THE EMPEROR AUGUSTUS (63 B.C.–A.D. 14)

He left Rome a city of marble, they said.
He'd found it a city of brick.
Whatever else you might think about him,
That's really a marvelous trick.

He won a great fight at Philippi, they said.
He put his opponents to shame.
He sent them all scurrying back to their mothers,
And won for himself lasting fame.

Augustus is pronounced aw-GUST-us. *Octavian* is pronounced ock-TAY-vee-un. *Philippi* is pronounced fill-LIP-eye.

He straightened out government problems, they said.
Encouraged artistic creation.
The very first emperor to rule over Rome,
Augustus caused quite a sensation.

Though his mother called him "Octavian,"
He later changed his name.
But "Augustus" or "Octavian"
His glory is the same.

GALEN (A.D. 29–about 210)

Galen was a doctor,
A man of science, too.
His patients bragged about his skills.
His reputation grew.

Five hundred books—all medical—
He wrote to let folks know
The structure of anatomy—
Where everything should go.

The working of the arteries
Was just one thing he taught.
He showed that they were full of blood,
Not air, as folks had thought.

He wrote about the heart and pulse,
The spinal cord and brain,
How to cool a fever,
How to stop a pain.

For at least a thousand years,
His teachings were the rule.
(Back then a doctor didn't have
To graduate from school.)

Galen is pronounced GAY-lin. Although Galen was born in Greece, he moved to Rome, where he practiced his medical skills.

CICERO (106–43 B.C.)

Cicero, Cicero, speaker sublime

Accused the conspirator named Catiline.

He opposed Julius Caesar,

Mark Antony too.

His problems with powerful enemies grew.

They had him killed,

He died all alone.

His great speeches meant

He would always be known.

Cicero is pronounced SIS-er-o. *Catiline* is pronounced CAT-ill-line.

41

ADRIAN'S WALL

In England years and years ago, the Romans looked about.
It really was a lovely place to live, without a doubt.
But still the soldiers worried over danger from attacks.
(Soldiers in the military have to watch their backs.)

The soldiers said to Hadrian, the emperor of all Rome,
"We need some more protection here so we'll be safe at home."
They said, "A wall is what we need to set our minds at rest,
A wall that's long and thick and strong to withstand every test."
Said Hadrian, "It's clear to me you're absolutely right.
We need a wall to keep you safe when you're asleep at night."

The structure that they built was very tall and very wide
It cut the country right in half; they viewed their work with pride.
The wall went on for miles and miles, sturdy, strong, and stout.
The soldiers then could sleep at night. Their foes were all kept out.

Hadrian is pronounced HAY-dree-an. Hadrian's Wall is 73.5 miles (118 kilometers) long. It was built between A.D. 122 and 126. It was about 20 feet (6 meters) high and 8 feet (2.4 meters) thick. Parts of it are still standing.

HE FALL OF ROME

"Barbarians"
Rome called the tribes
Who lived beyond its borders.
Rome conquered them,
Destroyed their towns.
Then Rome gave all the orders.

But years went by
And Rome grew weak.
Barbarians grew stronger.
At last there came
The bitter time
Rome ruled the world no longer.

Barbarians
Poured into Rome.
They looted, burned, and killed.
The way of life
That once was Rome
Was now forever stilled.

MORE ABOUT ANCIENT ROME

Books

MacDonald, Fiona. *Women in Ancient Rome.* Chicago: NTC/Contemporary Publishing, 2000.

McKeever, Susan. *Ancient Rome.* New York: Dorling Kindersley, 1995.

Rees, Rosemary. *The Ancient Romans.* Chicago: Heinemann Library, 1999.

Watkins, Richard Ross. *Gladiator.* New York: Houghton Mifflin, 1997.

Websites

The Christian Catacombs of Rome
http://www.catacombe.roma.it/
Learn about underground Roman passageways from a website from the Salesiano Institute in San Callisto, Rome

Roman Art
http://www.dia.org/collections/ancient/rome/rome.html
View pieces of ancient Roman artwork, such as sculptures held by the Detroit Institute of Arts

Map of Ancient Rome
http://www.lib.utexas.edu/Libs/PCL/Map_collection/historical/Peutingerian_Tables_A.D.393.jpg
See a map of Ancient Rome from the University of Texas archives

Odyssey Online: Rome
http://www.emory.edu/CARLOS/ODYSSEY/ROME/homepg.html
Learn about Ancient Rome from a website sponsored in part by Emory University and the University of Rochester

Secrets of Lost Empires: Roman Baths
http://www.pbs.org/wgbh/nova/lostempires/roman/
Find out about the Roman baths from NOVA Online

INDEX

ABOUT THE AUTHORS

Susan Altman and **Susan Lechner**, both graduates of Wellesley College, currently produce the Emmy Award–winning television program *It's Academic* in Washington, D.C., and Baltimore, Maryland. They have also produced *It's Elementary, Heads Up!,* and *Pick Up the Beat.* They are coauthors of *Followers of the North Star,* a book of rhymes for young people (also published by Children's Press). Ms. Altman is also the author of the play *Out of the Whirlwind* and the books *Extraordinary African-Americans* and *The Encyclopedia of African-American Heritage.*